HAWAII

The Aloha State

BY
JOHN HAMILTON

Abdo & Daughters

An imprint of Abdo Publishing | abdopublishing.com

abdopublishing.com

Published by ABDO Publishing, a division of ABDO, PO Box 398166, Minneapolis, Minnesota 55439. Copyright © 2017 by Abdo Consulting Group, Inc. International copyrights reserved in all countries. No part of this book may be reproduced in any form without written permission from the publisher. ABDO & Daughters™ is a trademark and logo of ABDO Publishing.

Printed in the United States of America, North Mankato, Minnesota.
012016
092016

THIS BOOK CONTAINS
RECYCLED MATERIALS

Editor: Sue Hamilton   **Contributing Editor:** Bridget O'Brien
Graphic Design: Sue Hamilton
Cover Art Direction: Candice Keimig   **Cover Photo Selection:** Neil Klinepier
Cover Photo: iStock
Interior Images: Alamy, AP, Bishop Museum, Corbis, Dreamstime, Getty, Granger, Hawaii State Archives, Herb Kane, History in Full Color-Restoration/Colorization, Honolulu International Airport, Hormel Foods, iStock, John Webber, Library of Congress, Mile High Maps, National Park Service, One Mile Up, NASA, NOAA Coastal Services Center, RavenFire, ThinkStock, U.S. Navy, Waikiki Spam Jam, White House, & Wikimedia.

Statistics: *State and City Populations*, U.S. Census Bureau, July 1, 2014 estimates; *Land and Water Area*, U.S. Census Bureau, 2010 Census, MAF/TIGER database; *State Temperature Extremes*, NOAA National Climatic Data Center; *Climatology and Average Annual Precipitation*, NOAA National Climatic Data Center, 1980-2015 statewide averages; *State Highest and Lowest Points*, NOAA National Geodetic Survey.

Websites: To learn more about the United States, visit booklinks.abdopublishing.com. These links are routinely monitored and updated to provide the most current information available.

Cataloging-in-Publication Data

Names: Hamilton, John, 1959- author.
Title: Hawaii / by John Hamilton.
Description: Minneapolis, MN : Abdo Publishing, [2016] | The United States of America | Includes index.
Identifiers: LCCN 2015957537 | ISBN 9781680783131 (print) | ISBN 9781680774177 (ebook)
Subjects: LCSH: Hawaii--Juvenile literature.
Classification: DDC 996.9--dc23
LC record available at http://lccn.loc.gov/2015957537

CONTENTS

THE ALOHA STATE

Hawaii is like a string of emerald jewels that stretch across the deep blue sea. Author Mark Twain once wrote that Hawaii was the "loveliest fleet of islands that lies anchored in any ocean." This chain of volcanic islands is called a tropical paradise for good reason. Nestled in the middle of the Pacific Ocean, it is a place of breathtaking beauty.

In Hawaii, people bask in the warm climate while marveling at the state's sandy beaches, towering mountains, lush forests, waterfalls, and rainbows. But Hawaii's most precious resource is its people. Many ethnic groups blend together, bound by their tropical island home.

Hawaii's nickname is "The Aloha State." The word "aloha" is Hawaiian. It means both "hello" and "goodbye." It can also mean "peace" and "compassion." This perfectly reflects the warm and friendly spirit of Hawaii.

Kilauea is an active volcano on Hawaii's Big Island.

QUICK
FACTS

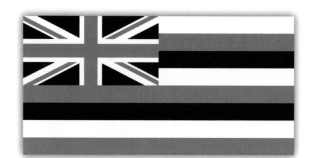

Name: The name "Hawaii" may be related to the Polynesian word "Hawaiki," which means "homeland." The name might also refer to the Polynesian folklore legend Hawai'iloa, who discovered the islands.

State Capital: Honolulu, population 350,399

Date of Statehood: August 21, 1959 (50th state)

Population: 1,419,561 (40th-most populous state)

Area (Total Land and Water): 10,932 square miles (28,314 sq km), 43rd-largest state

Largest City: Honolulu, population 350,399

Nickname: The Aloha State

Motto: *Ua Mau ke Ea o ka Aina i ka Pono* (The Life of the Land is Perpetuated in Righteousness)

State Bird: Nene (Hawaiian Goose)

State Flower: Yellow Hibiscus

State Gemstone: Black Coral

State Tree: Kukui, also called the Candlenut

State Song: "Hawaii Ponoi" ("Hawaii's Own")

Highest Point: Pu'u Wekiu Cinder Cone, Mauna Kea, 13,796 feet (4,205 m)

Lowest Point: Pacific Ocean, 0 feet (0 m)

Average July High Temperature: 86°F (30°C)

Record High Temperature: 100°F (38°C), at Pahala on April 27, 1931

Average January Low Temperature: 65°F (18°C)

Record Low Temperature: 12°F (-11°C), at Mauna Kea Observatory on May 17, 1979

Average Annual Precipitation: Varies from more than 450 inches (1,143 cm) in the mountains of Kauai, to less than 10 inches (25 cm) in the western lowlands on the island of Hawaii.

Number of U.S. Senators: 2

Number of U.S. Representatives: 2

U.S. Presidents Born in Hawaii: Barack Obama

U.S. Postal Service Abbreviation: HI

QUICK FACTS

GEOGRAPHY

The state of Hawaii is an archipelago (a group of islands). It is located in the central Pacific Ocean. There are 137 islands in the state. They stretch in a line that is 1,500 miles (2,414 km) long, with a total area of 10,932 square miles (28,314 sq km). About 6,423 square miles (16,635 sq km) of that is land area. Hawaii is roughly 2,400 miles (3,862 km) from the United States mainland. It is the southernmost state.

Most of Hawaii's islands are small and uninhabited. The eight largest islands, from northwest to southeast, include: Niihau, Kauai, Oahu, Molokai, Lanai, Maui, Kahoolawe, and the island of Hawaii (also called the Big Island). About 70 percent of Hawaii's population lives in or near the capital of Honolulu, on the island of Oahu.

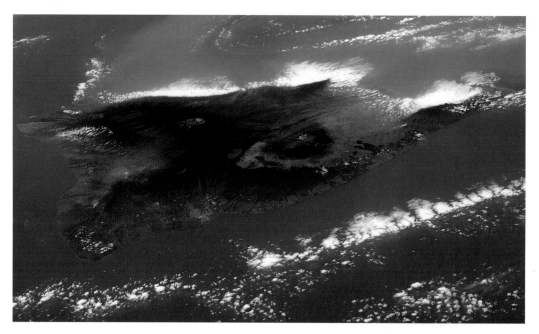

Hawaii's Big Island as viewed from the International Space Station.

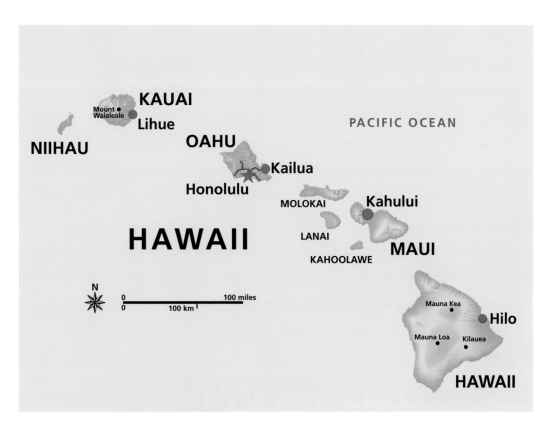

KAUAI
Mount Waialeale ●
Lihue
NIIHAU
OAHU
Kailua
Honolulu
PACIFIC OCEAN
MOLOKAI
Kahului
HAWAII
LANAI
KAHOOLAWE
MAUI
N
0   100 miles
0   100 km
Mauna Kea ●
Hilo
Mauna Loa ●   Kilauea ●
HAWAII

Hawaii

Pacific Ocean

Hawaii's total land and water area is 10,932 square miles (28,314 sq km). It is the 43rd-largest state. The state capital is Honolulu on the island of Oahu.

GEOGRAPHY

The Earth's crust is made of tectonic plates that cover the planet. These plates move slowly over millions of years. Sometimes volcanoes erupt in the middle of a plate. These eruptions are called hot spots. Millions of years ago, a hot spot formed on the bottom of the Pacific Ocean. Molten rock built up until it rose above the ocean surface. The magma eventually cooled, forming an island. Over time, the tectonic plate continued moving, but the hot spot stayed in the same position. A long string of islands formed, until the archipelago we call Hawaii was created.

Erosion began shaping the hardened lava. Strong waves caused rocks and sand to grind against each other, creating Hawaii's famous sandy beaches. Ocean currents and birds brought plant life, which took seed on the islands. Over millions of years, the tropical paradise we know today emerged.

Landforms of Hawaii
BY NOAA COASTAL SERVICES CENTER

Cultivated Agricultural Land

Upland Evergreen Forest

Upland Dry Scrub and Volcanic Soil

Incised and Eroded Canyon Landscape

Grassland and Rangeland

Bare Exposed Lava Flow

Tropical Rain Forest

High and Low Intensity Urban Development

Water erodes grooves on Kauai's Mount Waialeale. It is one of the wettest spots on Earth, receiving about 450 inches (1,143 cm) of rain per year.

Volcanoes are still active today on the Big Island of Hawaii. One of the biggest volcanoes on Earth is Mauna Loa. The Kilauea volcano is very active. It has been spewing lava since 1983, when its last eruption occurred.

Hawaii receives much rainfall in mountainous areas. Gushing water splashing downhill has eroded the lava and created beautiful valleys and grooves on the mountainsides.

The Wailuku River is located on the island of Hawaii. At 26 miles (42 km) in length, it is the longest river in the state.

GEOGRAPHY

CLIMATE AND
WEATHER

Hawaii is famous for its year-round pleasant weather. The state has a tropical climate. Fresh ocean breezes from the east (called trade winds) keep Hawaii's temperatures mild and steady. Along the coasts, the temperature rarely climbs above 90°F (32°C) or dips below 65°F (18°C). In the high mountains, temperatures can be much colder. Winter snows often cover the summit of Mauna Kea on the island of Hawaii. (In Hawaiian, Mauna Kea means "White Mountain.")

Hawaii has two seasons, although they are similar. The "winter" wet season lasts from October to April. Moisture-laden trade winds drop much rain on the windward, east-facing, side of the islands. The leeward, west-facing, sides are drier. During the "summer" dry season, the islands get less rain, although showers are still common.

Hawaii is known for its pleasant tropical climate. Tourists and residents enjoy fresh ocean breezes and mild, steady temperatures.

Hawaii's rainfall amounts vary greatly. On the island of Kauai, Mount Waialeale is one of the rainiest places on the planet. It averages more than 450 inches (1,143 cm) of rainfall each year. On the other hand, places along the western side of the Big Island of Hawaii average less than 10 inches (25 cm) of rain per year.

Tropical storms sometimes lash Hawaii. They bring high winds and much rain. Hurricane season lasts from June through November, although these strong storms rarely strike the islands.

PLANTS AND
ANIMALS

Forests cover almost half of Hawaii. In areas with rich soil and much rain, there is dense tropical growth. Ferns, flowering plants, and towering trees are common. In drier parts of the islands, grasslands and pastures cover the land.

Hawaii is a chain of volcanic islands surrounded by the vast Pacific Ocean. It has many unique plants. How did they get there? Their seeds and pollen arrived long ago by hitchhiking on seafaring birds. Ocean currents and winds brought more plant life. After millions of years, the plants evolved and became endemic, or unique, to Hawaii. Today, Hawaii has about 1,400 plants that are found nowhere else on Earth.

Fragrant and sturdy plumeria flowers are found all over Hawaii.

Native and non-native plants and trees flourish in Hawaii's warm, tropical climate. Many types of orchids are grown and used to make leis, the popular flower necklaces worn on the islands. But only three orchid species are native to Hawaii.

When humans first traveled to Hawaii about 1,700 years ago, they brought many kinds of plants with them to the islands. When Europeans and Americans began settling in Hawaii in the 1800s, they also brought along many non-native plants and trees. Oleanders, orchids, and cash crops such as sugarcane and pineapple are not native to Hawaii. These and other non-native species have crowded out unique Hawaiian plants. Many native plants have become extinct or endangered.

PLANTS AND ANIMALS

Hoary Bat

Monk Seal

There are many kinds of fruits and root plants in Hawaii. They include coconuts, sweet potatoes, bananas, sugarcane, taro, and breadfruit. Hawaii is famous for its large variety of flowering plants. These include fragrant and colorful orchids. The state flower is the yellow hibiscus.

A huge variety of trees grow on the islands. They include palms, koas, hapuu tree ferns, monkeypods, banyans, mangos, albizias, and ohias. The state tree is the candlenut. Also known as the kukui tree, its oil is used in dyes and candles.

There are only two mammals that are native to Hawaii. Both are endangered today. Hawaiian hoary bats have brown fur that has a "frosty" appearance. They are found on the islands of Hawaii and Kauai. Hawaiian monk seals like to hunt for fish and lobsters.

Green Sea Turtle

As people settled Hawaii, they brought other animals with them to the islands. These included deer, goats, rats, and mongooses. Common Hawaiian reptiles include geckos, frogs, toads, lizards, and turtles.

Many kinds of birds are found throughout Hawaii. They include honeycreepers, elepaios, Hawaiian hawks, finches, sparrows, cardinals, and doves. Coastal birds include terns, frigate birds, albatrosses, petrels, and shearwaters. The nene, or Hawaiian goose, is the official state bird.

The ocean waters surrounding Hawaii teem with life. Deepwater fish include mackerel, snapper, tuna, marlin, and swordfish. Marine mammals include humpback whales and bottlenose dolphins. Endangered sea turtles are sometimes seen on Hawaii's beaches.

HISTORY

The earliest people came to Hawaii sometime between 300 AD and 700 AD. They were Polynesians from the Marquesas Islands, south of Hawaii. They traveled more than 2,300 miles (3,701 km) in large canoes across

Polynesians sailed across the Pacific Ocean to Hawaii.

the stormy Pacific Ocean. By about 1000 AD, another wave of people arrived on the islands. They were from the Polynesian island of Tahiti. Many historians think the Polynesians called their new home "Hawaiki." It is a Polynesian word that means "homeland." Today we call it Hawaii.

Because the islands are so remote, the new settlers formed their own culture. They lived in villages. Their houses were made of wood and woven grass. They raised chickens and pigs brought from Polynesia. They also brought bananas, sugarcane, and other crops. They grew a root called taro. It was baked and ground into a pudding called poi. They caught fish from the sea with hand-woven nets.

Carved wooden figures known as tikis represent Hawaiian gods. These tikis stand in the Pu `uhonua O Honaunau National Historical Park in Hawaii.

The Hawaiians developed a religion with many gods and goddesses. Pele was a powerful goddess who lived in the volcano Kilauea, on the Big Island of Hawaii. The people carved wooden figures called tikis to represent their gods.

Throughout the islands, there were many kingdoms. Each had its own chief. These groups often fought with each other. They competed for land and natural resources.

Captain Cook and his crew meet native Hawaiians off today's Kauai in 1778.

The first Europeans to visit Hawaii were led by British explorer Captain James Cook. His expedition landed at Waimea on the island of Kauai in 1778. They came in two large sailing ships, the HMS *Resolution* and HMS *Discovery*.

Captain Cook named the new land the "Sandwich Islands." This honored British statesman John Montagu, the 4th Earl of Sandwich. Montagu helped raise money for the expedition. (Montagu also "invented" (or at least made popular) the modern lunch dish consisting of meat placed between two slices of bread.) Later, the name "Sandwich Islands" was replaced by "Hawaiian Islands," or simply Hawaii.

The following year, Captain Cook returned to Hawaii. This time, the expedition landed on the Big Island. Cultural misunderstandings erupted between the British and the Hawaiians. On February 14, 1779, Captain Cook was killed in a battle at Kealakekua Bay.

Captain Cook's expedition made Hawaii well known. Soon, traders and settlers from Europe and the United States began visiting the islands. American whaling ships spent time resupplying in Hawaii's tropical ports.

Starting in the 1780s, the islands were plunged into a series of wars between the rival chiefs. King Kamehameha the Great united all the warring tribes. He established the Kingdom of Hawaii in 1810.

Contact with Europeans and Americans brought tragedy to the native Hawaiians. Their culture began to change. Worse, the Hawaiians had no resistance to diseases such as smallpox and influenza. By the early 1800s, disease and warfare between rival tribes killed thousands of native Hawaiians.

KAMEHAMEHA I

HISTORY

Christian missionaries from New England first arrived in Hawaii in 1820. They brought modern culture to the islands, but the native Hawaiians lost many of their traditions.

People from the United States began buying land and growing sugarcane. Large plantations hired many workers from Japan, China, and other countries. That is one reason why today's Hawaii has so many people from different cultures.

Sanford Dole (standing, white beard) was president of the Republic of Hawaii and later the first governor of the Territory of Hawaii.

Tension grew between native Hawaiians and the rich landowners. The sugarcane growers feared that the Hawaiian leaders were not governing the country in a way that benefited wealthy residents. In 1893, with help from a group of U.S. Marines, a group of businessmen seized control. They created a new Republic of Hawaii in 1894. Sanford Dole was its first president.

The armed takeover of Hawaii was very controversial. The people who controlled the government wanted the island nation to become a territory of the United States. That did not happen at first. But in just a few years, newly elected U.S. President William McKinley annexed Hawaii in 1898.

The USS *Shaw* explodes during the Japanese attack on Pearl Harbor in 1941.

On December 7, 1941, Japanese warplanes attacked the U.S. military base at Pearl Harbor on the island of Oahu. The attack caused the United States to enter World War II. Military bases on Hawaii continued to be important, even after the war ended in 1945.

On August 21, 1959, Hawaii became the 50th state. Military spending and the growing of sugarcane and pineapples boosted the state's economy. In recent decades, tourism has become the most important single part of Hawaii's economy.

HISTORY

DID YOU KNOW?

- Pele is the goddess of volcanoes, fire, lightning, and wind in the Hawaiian religion. She is said to have created the islands of Hawaii. She lives in Kilauea volcano on the Big Island of Hawaii. She is very powerful, and can be dangerously moody. Some people believe that when tourists take volcanic rocks home as souvenirs, they anger Pele and bring bad luck.

- Spam is a canned meat product made by Hormel Foods. It is more popular in Hawaii than any other state. First introduced in the islands during World War II, today almost seven million cans of Spam are eaten each year in Hawaii. Spam even has its own food festival. The Waikiki Spam Jam is held each year in Honolulu.

- More than 70 percent of Hawaiians, nearly one million people, live on the island of Oahu. About 4 of 10 people on Oahu live in the state capital of Honolulu. Oahu has dozens of sandy beaches for surfing, swimming, and snorkeling, including legendary Waikiki Beach.

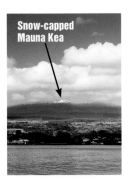

Snow-capped Mauna Kea

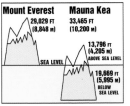

Mount Everest
29,029 FT
(8,848 M)

Mauna Kea
33,465 FT
(10,200 M)

13,796 FT
(4,205 M)
ABOVE SEA LEVEL

SEA LEVEL

19,669 FT
(5,995 M)
BELOW
SEA LEVEL

- The largest island in the state of Hawaii is called Hawaii. It is nicknamed the Big Island so that people can tell it apart from the state. It is larger than all the other Hawaiian Islands combined. At its widest point, it is 93 miles (150 km) across. Its highest point is the dormant volcano Mauna Kea. Sometimes capped with snow, the mountain is 13,796 feet (4,205 m) high. But measured from its base *under* the Pacific Ocean, it soars more than 33,000 feet (10,058 m), which is taller than Mount Everest.

Yellow-Bellied Sea Snake

Blind Snake

- It is a myth that there are no snakes on Hawaii. Two species are found regularly in the state. Yellow-bellied sea snakes are highly venomous. Luckily, people rarely encounter them. They are most common in the waters around the smaller uninhabited islands of the northwest. Island blind snakes are harmless. They are about the size of earthworms. Islanders are always on the lookout for invasive snakes, such as illegal pet boa constrictors. In large numbers, invasive snakes could devastate Hawaii's delicate ecosystem.

- The island of Kauai is home to Waimea Canyon. This colorful gorge is called "The Grand Canyon of the Pacific." It is 14 miles (23 km) long and more than 3,600 feet (1,097 m) deep.

DID YOU KNOW?

PEOPLE

Barack Obama (1961-) served as the 44th president of the United States. He was president for two terms, serving from 2009 to 2017. He was born in Honolulu, Hawaii. Obama's mother was from Kansas, and his father was from Kenya, Africa. After graduating from Columbia University in New York, he worked as a community organizer in Chicago, Illinois, helping people train for work. He graduated from Harvard Law School in Massachusetts in 1991. He was elected to the United States Senate in 2004.

As president of the United States, Obama helped the country recover from the worst economic downturn since the Great Depression of the 1930s. He pushed for laws that helped ordinary Americans, including tax and health care reform.

Kamehameha I (1758?-1819) was the first king to unite the Hawaiian Islands. Through treaties and warfare, he combined the many warring tribes of Hawaii into one government in the late 1700s and early 1800s. Also called Kamehameha the Great, he became the ruler of the Kingdom of Hawaii in 1810. During his reign, he worked to keep Hawaii independent and to preserve its unique culture.

Liliuokalani (1838-1917) was the last monarch of the Kingdom of Hawaii. She ruled as queen starting in 1891. She tried to pass a new constitution restoring voting rights to poor Hawaiians. The kingdom was overthrown in 1893 by a group of Americans. Queen Liliuokalani surrendered to avoid warfare.

Bethany Hamilton (1990-) is a competitive surfer. She started surfing at age eight. In 2003, she survived a shark attack that took her left arm. After recovering from her injury, she continued surfing and returned to competition in 2004. Hamilton was born and raised on the island of Kauai.

Duke Kahanamoku (1890-1968) was born in Honolulu, Oahu. Competing in three different Olympic Games in 1912, 1920, and 1924, he won a total of three gold and two silver medals in swimming. He also popularized surfing worldwide. He is in the Swimming Hall of Fame, the Surfing Hall of Fame, and the U.S. Olympic Hall of Fame.

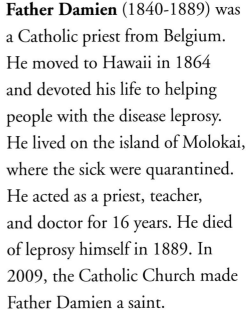

Father Damien (1840-1889) was a Catholic priest from Belgium. He moved to Hawaii in 1864 and devoted his life to helping people with the disease leprosy. He lived on the island of Molokai, where the sick were quarantined. He acted as a priest, teacher, and doctor for 16 years. He died of leprosy himself in 1889. In 2009, the Catholic Church made Father Damien a saint.

Don Ho (1930-2007) was a Hawaiian singer, musician, and entertainer. He brought humor and a sweet interpretation to Hawaiian songs and other music. Through television and traveling stage shows, he helped make Hawaii a popular tourist destination. His shows were always filled with songs, jokes, and Hawaiian history. He sold millions of records worldwide. Two of his most famous songs were "Tiny Bubbles" and "I'll Remember You." Don Ho was born in Honolulu.

CITIES

Honolulu is the capital of Hawaii. It is on the southeast side of the island of Oahu. Its population is 350,399. Combined with nearby communities, it is home to about one million residents. People have lived in the area for almost 1,000 years. King Kamehameha I moved his royal court to Honolulu in 1809. Today, the city is a gateway to the rest of the state. Most air and ship traffic that comes to Hawaii first enters through Honolulu. The city is a center for trade, government, the military, and tourism. There are many sandy beaches, including world-famous Waikiki Beach. Several universities are located in Honolulu, including the University of Hawaii at Manoa.

Kailua is on the east coast of Oahu, about a 30-minute drive from Honolulu's Waikiki Beach. Kailua's name means "two seas." One part of the city contains two large lagoons separated by a peninsula. People have lived in the area for about 1,500 years. Kailua Beach is one of the most beautiful beaches in the world. The sandy, crescent-shaped beach is a big tourist attraction. Steady trade winds make the beach popular with windsurfers. President Barack Obama often took winter vacations in the city. About 36,000 people live in Kailua.

Hilo is the largest city on the Big Island of Hawaii. Its population is about 41,000. The city wraps around Hilo Bay, on the east side of the island. Early settlers came to the area about 900 years ago. They made their living farming and fishing. Today, the city is home to the University of Hawaii at Hilo. There are many waterfalls and flower gardens in Hilo. The city's art galleries and museums attract many tourists. In addition, Hilo is the gateway to Hawaii Volcanoes National Park.

Kahului is on the north coast of Maui. It was a center for sugar production starting in the mid-1800s. Today, with a population of about 26,000, it is the biggest city on the island. It has an airport and deepwater harbor. It is also a retail center for island residents.

Lihue is on the southeastern coast of the "Garden Isle" of Kauai. It was first settled by native Hawaiians about 1,000 years ago. Today, the city has about 6,500 residents. Tourism is the largest industry on Kauai. Lihue has many resorts, golf clubs, sandy beaches, and attractions such as nearby Wailua Falls. Lihue is also home to Kauai's main airport.

TRANSPORTATION

Because Hawaii is a collection of islands in the middle of the Pacific Ocean, ships and airplanes are very important for the state's transportation needs.

Each Hawaiian island has ports for ocean transportation. The busiest harbor is at Honolulu, on the island of Oahu. Large, oceangoing ships take products out of Hawaii to ports around the world. Most goods coming into Hawaii also go through Honolulu Harbor. The harbor is also a busy cruise ship terminal.

When people come to Hawaii, most pass through busy Honolulu International Airport. With four active runways, the airport serves more than 20 million visitors each year. Built on the waterfront near downtown Honolulu, it is one of the most beautiful airports in the world. After flying to Honolulu, many visitors then take "island hopper" flights to other islands, which have smaller airports.

Honolulu International Airport

Hawaii has about 4,430 miles (7,129 km) of public roads. State highways circle each island. The only federal interstate highways are on Oahu. Interstate H-1 passes through Honolulu and surrounding communities. Interstate H-2 travels north from Pearl City to the city of Wahiawa. Interstate H-3 (shown here) runs eastward from Pearl Harbor, through a series of tunnels under a mountain range, and ends on the east coast at Marine Corps Base Hawaii. It is one of the most expensive interstate highways ever constructed.

NATURAL RESOURCES

There are no important minerals mined in Hawaii. There are some gravel and sand quarries. Energy-making oil and coal must be imported from the mainland. Wind power is becoming a major way of generating electricity in the state.

Hawaii's rich, volcanic soil is well suited for farming. A large variety of crops are grown on Hawaii's 7,500 farms and plantations. The most valuable crops include sugarcane, macadamia nuts, mangoes, coffee, bananas, and papayas. Most of the harvest is sold and exported to the United States mainland and other countries.

James Dole started the first pineapple plantation and packing plant on Oahu in 1901. By the early 1920s, Dole's company had become the largest pineapple packer in the world. Other companies, such as Del Monte, joined Dole in growing millions of pineapples on vast acreages of Hawaiian land. The state continued to dominate worldwide pineapple production until the end of the 20th century. Competition from other countries caused the market for Hawaiian pineapples to collapse. Today, fresh pineapples grown in Hawaii are mostly sold for state residents to eat.

Pineapple

A cattle ranch on the island of Oahu.

Besides growing crops, some Hawaiian land is also used to raise beef cattle, hogs, dairy cows, and chickens. Most large ranches are on the Big Island of Hawaii. Hawaiian cowboys learned to ride horses and manage cattle herds from Mexican vaqueros in the 1830s.

Hawaii has a limited commercial fishing industry. The most valuable catch by far is skipjack and yellowfin tuna, followed by swordfish, blue marlin, snapper, sea bass, and mahimahi.

Yellowfin tuna for sale at a fish market in Hawaii.

NATURAL RESOURCES

INDUSTRY

Hawaii's economy has changed much during its history. In the 1800s, the biggest industries were whaling and the harvesting of sandalwood. In the early 1900s, the growing and packing of pineapples and sugarcane dominated.

Today, tourism is the single biggest industry on the islands. In 2013, about 8 million tourists spent $14.5 billion in Hawaii, supporting nearly 168,000 jobs. Most visitors come from the United States mainland. Many also arrive from Canada, Australia, and Japan. They come to enjoy Hawaii's pleasant climate, beaches, shopping, and recreational activities.

Tourists get surfing instruction on Waikiki Beach, Oahu, Hawaii.

United States sailors welcome a Japanese training squadron ship to Joint Base Pearl Harbor-Hickam. U.S. military bases are a major source of income to Hawaii's state economy.

The United States government greatly helps Hawaii's economy. There are several military bases currently on the islands. They employ many Hawaiians, and military personnel spend money at state businesses. Hawaiian military bases include Joint Base Pearl Harbor-Hickam in Oahu, Schofield Barracks Army Base in Oahu, Marine Corps Base Hawaii in Oahu, Station Maui Coast Guard Base in Maui, and Pacific Missile Range Facility Barking Sands in Kauai.

Hawaiian manufacturing companies are found mainly in Oahu. They use raw materials mostly imported from the United States mainland. Hawaiian factories make products such as clothing, cement, and chemicals. Food manufacturing is a smaller part of today's Hawaiian economy, but factories continue to produce products such as canned pineapple, fish, and sugar.

INDUSTRY

SPORTS

Hawaii is often called the birthplace of surfing. Early Polynesians brought the sport to Hawaii hundreds of years ago. They first surfed on big wooden planks. Duke Kahanamoku is called "The Father of Modern Surfing." He was an Olympic medal-winning swimmer who helped make the sport popular in the early 1900s. Today, it is enjoyed by millions of people worldwide. Surfing competitions are held each year in Hawaii, especially on Oahu's North Shore, where big waves arrive in winter.

Besides surfing, Hawaii offers many other activities for outdoor lovers. The state's mild climate makes it perfect for golfing, mountain hiking, tennis, swimming, boating, and diving. Skiing and snowboarding are possible in the winter months atop snow-capped Mauna Kea volcano on the Big Island.

There are no professional major league sports teams in Hawaii. However, the National Football League often plays its Pro Bowl all-star game at Aloha Stadium in Honolulu, Oahu. The Hawaii Bowl is a postseason college football game held each December. Sports teams from the University of Hawaii are very popular statewide.

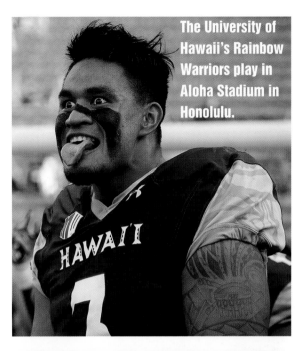

The University of Hawaii's Rainbow Warriors play in Aloha Stadium in Honolulu.

Athletes start a World Ironman Triathlon Championship on Hawaii's Big Island. Competitors swim 2.4 miles (3.8 km), then bike for 112 miles (180 km), and finally run for 26.2 miles (42 km). They have a time limit of 17 hours to complete the race.

Major professional golf tournaments are held on Oahu, Maui, and Kauai. The World Ironman Triathlon Championship is held each year on the Big Island of Hawaii. Each December, the Honolulu Marathon draws thousands of long-distance runners to Oahu.

ENTERTAINMENT

Hawaii contains a mix of different cultures. There is a strong Asian influence in the state, especially from Japan. Many of Hawaii's best museums and art galleries highlight the state's cultural heritage. The Honolulu Museum of Art was founded in 1922. It contains more than 50,000 works of art, including many pieces from Hawaiian and Asian artists.

A luau is a feast that includes traditional Hawaiian food along with music, hula dancing, and other entertainment. Common food served at luaus includes roast pig, poi, tropical fruit, and Hawaiian sweet potatoes. Diners wear leis (necklaces of flowers). Music includes drums and ukuleles, which resemble small guitars.

People at Hawaii Volcanoes National Park watch as lava from Kilauea oozes toward the Pacific Ocean.

The USS *Arizona* Memorial is in Pearl Harbor in Honolulu, Oahu. It commemorates the final resting place of the United States battleship *Arizona*, which sank during a Japanese attack on December 7, 1941. More than 1,100 of the Navy ship's sailors and Marines lost their lives. Today, the memorial is visited by more than two million people each year.

For visitors who like the outdoors, there are many beaches, hiking paths, and roads to travel on all the islands. There are two national parks in Hawaii. Haleakala National Park in Maui combines volcanic landscapes with sub-tropical rainforests. Hawaii Volcanoes National Park is on the Big Island of Hawaii.

TIMELINE

300 to 700 AD—The first people come to Hawaii from the Marquesas Islands.

About 1000 AD—More settlers arrive in Hawaii from Tahiti.

1778—British explorer Captain James Cook lands in Hawaii.

1810—King Kamehameha I unites all the tribes, establishing the Kingdom of Hawaii.

1820—The first Christian missionaries arrive on the islands.

1864—Father Damien moves to Hawaii. Nine years later, he moves to the island of Molokai and devotes his life to helping people with leprosy.

1893—United States representatives and colonists seize control of the islands. Queen Liliuokalani surrenders.

1898—Hawaii becomes an official territory of the United States.

1941—Japanese warplanes attack the U.S. military base at Pearl Harbor. The United States enters World War II.

1959—Hawaii becomes the 50th state of the United States.

1966—Hawaiian entertainer Don Ho releases "Tiny Bubbles." It becomes his most famous song, staying on Pop and Easy Listening charts for nearly a year.

1980—The first of 30 consecutive National Football League all-star Pro Bowl games is held in Aloha Stadium in Honolulu, Hawaii.

2009—Hawaii native Barack Obama becomes the 44th president of the United States.

GLOSSARY

Leprosy

A disease that causes disfiguring skin sores, nerve damage, and muscle weakness. People with the disease are known as lepers. A person with leprosy may give it to another person. Because of this, people with the disease were often sent to live in colonies, places where only other lepers lived. For example, the island of Molokai once had a leper colony. Today, medicines exist to treat leprosy, so isolating infected people is unnecessary.

Luau

A traditional Hawaiian feast.

Marquesas Islands

Islands about 2,000 miles (3,219 km) south of Hawaii. These islands are the homeland of the first Hawaiian settlers.

Missionary

A person sent on a mission to teach a religion or to help people in their everyday lives.

New England

An area of the United States that refers to the states of Connecticut, Maine, Massachusetts, New Hampshire, Rhode Island, and Vermont. People from this area are often called New Englanders.

Poi

A native Hawaiian food made by mixing taro root with water, cooking it, then pounding it into a paste. Poi may be eaten right away or allowed to sit for several days for a more sour flavor.

Polynesia

A region of the central and southern Pacific Ocean that contains more than 1,000 islands. Some of the islands include Hawaii, Samoa, New Zealand, Tahiti, and Tonga.

Tahiti

An island south of Hawaii, and east of Australia. People from Tahiti helped to settle Hawaii.

Taro

A root that was an important food source for the early people of Hawaii.

Ukulele

A four-stringed musical instrument shaped like a small guitar. It is used in many popular Hawaiian tunes.

Vaquero

Horsemen from Mexico who herded livestock, usually cattle. Many of their traditions were brought from Spain. Vaquero skills were adopted by cowboys of the American West.

World War II

A conflict that was fought from 1939 to 1945, involving countries around the world. The United States entered the war after Japan bombed the American naval base at Pearl Harbor, in Oahu, Hawaii, on December 7, 1941.

INDEX